Hedge Fund

& Other Living Margins

Hedge Fund

& Other Living Margins

Helen Moore

Shearsman Books

First published in the United Kingdom in 2012 by
Shearsman Books
50 Westons Hill Drive, Emersons Green
Bristol BS16 7DF

Shearsman Books Ltd Registered Office
30–31 St. James Place, Mangotsfield, Bristol BS16 9JB
(this address not for correspondence)

http://www.shearsman.com/

ISBN 978-1-84861-201-3

Acknowledgements
Some of these poems have appeared in *Magma, The Wolf, Tears in the
Fence, PAN* (Philosophy, Activism, Nature), Ecozon@ (Ecocritical
Journal), *Artemis Poetry, International Times, The Recusant, The Nail,
Green Spirit, Indra's Net, The Source, Buzz* (Templar Poetry), *In the
Telling* (Cinnamon Press), *Soul of the Earth* (Awen Publishing), *The
William Blake Birthday Book* (Bow of Burning Gold), *Emergency Verse*
(The Recusant), and *Anarchism and Sexuality: Ethics, Relationships and
Power* (Routledge).

I have also recorded a selection of the poems with musical responses
by Ken Masters and additional voice and bodhran by Niall McDevitt;
they feature on a CD entitled *Nature's Words: Selected Ecopoems 2*.

In addition to my collaborators, I would like to thank all those who
have critiqued or otherwise encouraged these poems, in particular
Electra Pinto, John Collins, Carrie Etter, Tim Liardet, Jay Ramsay,
Anthony Rudolf, Dikra Ridha, Lynnette Rees, Beverley Fergusson,
Anthony Nanson, Jenni Horsfall, Finally, I wish to honour three
guiding spirits, Rose Flint, Satish Kumar and—without whose love,
encouragement and editorial help this book may never
have come about—Niall McDevitt

Contents

Once upon a time, there was a hereafter.

—The Children

O children we are robbing! turn away!
May
we have left you not just dirt and dearth
on scrapheap Earth
but each of you the proud eye of a dream.

— Jonathan Griffin

The most remarkable feature of this historical moment on earth is not that we are on the way to destroying the world—we've actually been on the way for quite a while. It is that we are beginning to wake up, as from a millennia-long sleep, to a whole new relationship to our world, to ourselves and each other.

— Joanna Macy

Compassion is an act of imagination.

— Lindsay Clarke

...Change the myth in order to change the wider reality ... that is the way in which serious changes are eventually brought about.

— Mary Midgeley

Nature Story

Natural history—the lexical preserve of stretched skin, glass cases, curators in drab ties. Dusty, lifeless, atomised, it's Nature boiled down to a Whale's rib, air breathed through the dehumidifier's teeth.

It keeps neat accounts and classifications, but cannot imagine the latency of woodland, a fallen trunk rife with spores, the rhythms of Lichen. In its dreams the future's stuffed, and taxidermists rub their hands.

Hedge Fund

Little lines of sporting wood run wild
where hands heaved stones
to enclose—drove John Clare crazy.

Today those walls left to crumble—
cracking bark, and Hawthorn
boughs once plashed,
now ancient elbows' fold
and sinew; Hazel, Ash—
all create a delicate asylum.

Money markets usually lie
at the core of the financial
system, functioning quietly

Colonies of Snails,
feathers, crush of brittle
lime—a Song Thrush
sings up its midden.

Startled mouths—
White Dead Nettle flowers
open where a shot Fox
crept to die; here lies
minus an eye.

Maggots;
rubbing its feet a Fly—tip,
the yawn of a fridge;
Autumn leaves, debris
rots, spawns Hips and Haws
to feed the Songbirds and Badgers.

and so efficiently that they're
barely noticed. Like the human
heart, which beats continuously

A few bushes on,
the Elm where a Barn Owl
stared, burped its pellet—
grey ossuary of Mice,
Amen.

Still, Life finds its niches.
On rocks Lichens crottle,
and warty Elder stems
ooze with tar-black berries.
Below—cutting corners of tins,
and soft, ambulant Toads.

without conscious thought,
their global operation takes
place night and day, while

Gusts, tendrils—the scarlet fruit
of Woodbine flowers,
which lured Moths
on warm, moonlit evenings.

Glossy black plastic
stripped from silage;
Pheasants, beaters,
ha-ha,
shots, Retrievers;
coats hooked with Burdock;
shocks of electric wire.

a seizure of the market is like
a cardiac arrest, threatening
the orderly rhythm of the system

Dog Rose—thorns
like bloody fangs;
memories of blooms
that tea-cup Butterflies in June.

Cocoons, gossamer-stretch
between stems;
new risings of Ivy up old posts;
a Wren's nest tight as a child's fist;
Spindle, Holly;
and snagged on Bramble,
these newspaper flags.

on which the modern world
has come to depend. Now
it seems it's on life support—

Switch mechanical,
stink-horn diesel,
the implacable wheels and reach of a
tractor's machete. Random execution,
the insane-making crunch,
while the contractor sits
muffled in his cab,
on the wheel his hands
stiff as supermarket quotas…

share values in free-fall,
as investors predict their own
dwindling margins and returns.

Marginal, i

Very quaint, very Emily Dickinson, all those shouting nouns—
but how else to see sisters and brothers in margins and ghettos?

The Worst Winter in Thirty Years

A single Winter doesn't break
the pattern. O Fern frost,
iced webs, branch stipple-
engraved with Squirrel prints,
snow in swags and drifts
our kids had rarely seen.
Stillness, respite from
the relentless—
abandoned cars, time
to walk in wonder. Yet
hand-wringing, the calculated
loss to the economy, salt hills
dwindling, impasse, gritted
teeth. A single Winter
can break the bank.

Treasure Trove, *Survey of English Dialects, Northern Counties*

In a country of the past
a young Bird,
freshly shocked
from its shell,
was no standardised
date-stamped nestling,

but a bare-arse,
biddy, gollop,
bare-golling,
raw gorbet,
lile bird,
pudding kite,
red-raw kellick,
new hatched one.

A Wake to the Kittiwakes during London Fashion Week

A collage poem inspired by two articles juxtaposed in *The Guardian*, 16.9.06

Sprats are out this season
and Lerwick feels absolutely the new Cannes
now the North Sea's turned Mediterranean.
This is how it looks:

gaunt forms,
breast-bones protruding,
they strut and posture against a fabulous cliff-edge location—

and it's a muted palette:
Kittiwake white and grey
jostling Guillemot penguin suits,
with narrow neck-bands and those Cleopatra eyes,
o, and lots of retro ruffles,
feathers decidedly dishevelled.

An avian style of heroin chic,
it turns the spotters' heads
as the chicks lose their grip,
and, like Naomi on platform heels,
totter
and slip—

all
the
way
to double zero,
body-mass stripped,
make a splash where no flash-bulbs ever venture.

Bee

What do you feel
when you enter
the flower—

Love,
a lover,
a long, slow
linger of light?

The Fallen

A growing number of wildflower species are on the edge of extinction—
according to *The Vascular Plant Red Data List* 2005, nine native species
have been lost within the British Isles.

Here lies Ghost Orchid;
once haunted Beechwoods—
rest in peace.

Here lies Small Bur-parsley;
legion pot-herb of wastelands—
rest in peace.

Here lies Alpine Bladder-fern;
crosiers lost from damp highland rocks—
rest in peace.

Here lies Cottonweed;
assieged from Britain's beaches—
rest in peace.

Here lies Purple Spurge;
eternally procumbent—
rest in peace.

Here lies Marsh Fleawort;
ditched from fens, unrecorded—
rest in peace.

Here lies Downy Hemp-nettle;
the deceased passed unremarked from fields—
rest in peace.

Here lies Summer Lady's-tresses;
style totally outmoded—
rest in peace.

Here lies Lamb's Succory;
succumbed to high-yield wheat—
rest in peace.

And with each plant, its embedded companions,
the Unknown Biota lost to steady human pressure—
may your souls also rest in peace.

On Sisterhood and Service

The days of jam-traps have gone—
days of windfall plums perspiring under trees,
when my eyes would mutely rise to the water-line

to watch the Wasps drowning in the gloop;
jesters in their sticky black and yellow suits—feet
rubbing heads like siblings top-to-tail in bed.

Yesterday I heard a thin rasping, a sound
I hadn't heard in years, and tracing the saw's teeth
to the fence, I found a queen shaving wood for her nest.

Slowly the scene resurfaced, floating out its dregs—
the family meal, enjoying the season out of doors,
a linen cloth, those cadmium curls of tinned peaches,

pools of cream, Dad's flaps, Mum's screams;
the calm way I raised a knife like an impresario,
the mid-air swipe, and my astonishment

at the deadliness of my precision.
From its crescent abdomen the head and thorax
were severed off, but crawling in circles on the cloth

they became a foolhardy engine trying to recouple
with its derailed carriage—a freak show no one else
would witness. Nor did they wish to know

how a companion flew to her assistance, time and again
to raise her mutilated sister—fruitless attempts to right
what fear and mindless conjuring could never undo.

And o, the years trying to forget! But watching that secant queen, I saw a way to atone for my petty murder—my ear, my eye, my vocal chords would be of lifelong service.

Marginal, ii

Dog's Mercury—
Spring's quick-silver messenger,
canid wee flower.

Landscape as Dog Latrine

Dogs' breath on his neck,
an artist drives to the river-park,
opens the boot to release six hounds.
They lurch up the woodland path
eager to empty their bowels.

The artist follows behind
like a Chinese doctor stooping
to inspect the colour and texture
of their stools—they tell him nothing, but
are greatly pleasing to his eye—

the shape and chance placement,
the way the sunlight through the canopy
creates lunulae around and on them.
How this excrement will alter
with the passage of time, of pedestrians,
reveals the interest of the piece.

Since Marcel Duchamp
the latrine has gained iconic status
in the public's mind. In 'Fountain' lies
the apotheosis of the body's function,
ready-made by the civilised human,
but signed, of course, 'R. Mutt'.

The Unsung Pilchard

1. Song

We move as one,
many schools of thought, but one pelagic
principle, this throng going with the flow, cycles of Moon,
Sun; we, who once in our millions
were strong, swim on,
swim on,

through the cuff
and up the sleeve, La Manche/the English
Channel; down here territory is fleeting—no borders,
only sandbanks, shipwrecks, reefs;
the muddy phlegm
of a river

disgorging
into the marine; rocky outcrops of a stack
fractured from the land by breakers, Puffins scraping in its niches,
a common weal of Herring Gulls
shrieking for the lost
lands of Lyonesse;

the Celtic Sea,
and its abysmal gulf, where land's sedimental
shelf devolves to ocean, and gyres upwell planktonic soup to swell us,
but just enough—from land drift
the howls of Grey Seal pups
waiting, hungry…

Each sound
we know, each sea-mark as if our scales

bore maps, for these topographies are woven in the songs
of our species—*chants du poisson,*
these Piscean shanties
we learnt

in our nurseries.
They draw us, a single, steely bodkin
through the liquid seams; and sounding them we choir along,
a synchronised endeavour—leaderless,
but not without a rudder; we organise
to take our turn,

each elder
steering a course; then, flagging,
falling back to stream with brothers, sisters, who harmonising
as one, make this community one with the sea,
and this our only medium, for we
ichthyic Sheep,

a sea-locked flock
a forage crop, sacrifice our scales
to the greater whole, our comrades in the brine—Blue Shark
with large serrated jaws, Seals, Hake,
the southern-drawling Tunny…
swim on, swim on!

Night comes
and we migrate to moonlight,
the wavy top with Zooplankton as shimmered as our bellies.
Mouths and gill flaps open,
we buoy up to drink
the Eucharistic shine,

drink it with gratitude
to Manannan… Ma-na-nnan—mouthing
the syllables, we snack on Diatoms, ingest Copepods,
the salty titbits at the surface
who give their lives
that we may live.

Day breaks
and we shun the blinding Sun, go diving
through the columns of our basilica to escape the euphotic;
heads down we plunge towards
lugubrious Jellyfish,
benthic Rays.

Swim on
wild school, this *qui vive* of arrows
always a-quiver to deep tonal sounds, the vagaries of currents,
to changes in pressure, the warm
and cool pockets,
greys, greens

… and attack
from all sides—Shark, Seals, Hake,
Tunny, or bombing from above, Gannets snapping
at our staves, blowing us apart—
a thousand splinters
peeling away

to re-form
in altered alignment—some brothers,
sisters taken, but we, in all equanimity, accepting this kilter,
our gift being to balance
Life's creative tension…. Swim on,
swim on!

2. *Musyk*

Musyk hangs low over Porthmellin—days now with it pressing down, squeezing out the August Sun, which dribbles like the traine oil from an old Cornish lamp. Stoically the tourists nudge round little boats hauled up the slipway; a handful more bob in the harbour, their moorings shaggy arms that lift green hair, then set it back to soak.

An inquisitive visitor might peer into the gloom of net store and cellar, where fishwives once pressed Pilchards into crusts of salt, scales and blood. Another may eye the honeycomb of lobster-pots stacked against the granite walls; or the black plastic flags and footballs that seem to mark a funereal pastime. Mostly they stare out to sea, munching pasties, shooing teenage Gulls who mewl and cringe for crusts.

In former days fishermen were perched here along the quayside, busy patching sails, mending long lines and nets snagged by Sharks and Seals. Now the winch that wound the seine boats in—deck-boards slippy with sea-silver—has rusted up, cogs locked solid, a museum-piece of an almost extinct past.

*

Huer Mundy, born on Sunday, never liked a musyk occluding Mount's Bay. Still he can't miss a single day, walks these paths from harvest-time to Hallowe'en. Sharpest-eyed of all the local men, Mundy knows each trick of light, each trompe l'oeil the sea and sky can paint for him. He's read this Western Lizard more keenly than his Bible. From Carrag Luz to Mullion Cove, Predannack Cliff, Mên-te-heul to ghostly Ogo Dour, he knows each stream and inlet, the smugglers' caves when tides are low, roads where ships founder. Like a blind man he feels each inch of land, its rise and fall, feet steadfast between crags and boulders—these giant molars with their white and orange Lichens.

Beneath the whicker of Martins flicking for Flies, Mundy brushes Heather, catches his clothes on Bramble, Gorse, damp cobwebs woven through their thorns. But still his eyes comb the waves for signs heralding a school—diving Gannets, water crimson with the Pilchards' open gills. "Hevva! Hevva!" he shouts, "They're showing colour!" and raising his semaphore of bushes, he sends men quick as quilkins to their boats, hoisting sails, crewing out, while from their cottages, wives, children scurry to the cellars, sending up their cries and prayers for yet another bumper harvest.

Scrowlers galore… tuck-boats riding low, salt-spray, breakers pummelling kidneys, thighs, a bullion of prize-fighters. Toothed Wrack, and dragging at the men's legs, straps of Sea Thong, Devil Crabs, the limbs of the wrecked dead. On and on, tucking, scooping, shovelling, baskets and gurries bringing pounds, shillings, pence ashore…

3. Ditty

O thanks be to the Lord,
And thanks be to 'Is Lordship,
Who kindly grants the stems
For Porthmellin men to fish.

O, and the sea's indeed bountiful,
The Cornishmen strong,
And Chapel on a Sunday,
Teaches right from wrong.

And keep us from cholera,
Pray for our lives—
For the Lord and 'Is Lordship
Exact their cuts and tithes.

4. Dirge

Cruel cuts, quotas—Cornish, Welsh, Scottish fisher-folk
going out of business. Who makes a living from fishing? Ends
of long lines, men, whose fore-fathers lived from the sea, now
flounder, sign on once a week.

Reap without sowing,
sleep without knowing…

Marine creatures processed into food for humans, pets, poultry.
Fish factories, floating towns, construct economies of scale,
while trawlers scratch away insatiably to feed the industrial
maw. Maw, maw, maw! Electronic fish-finders send beams to
mine the Silver Pits for sterling, euros, dollars, their strange
yen for being caught, winched on board, popping eyes, and
mouths agape.

Reap without sowing,
sleep without knowing…

Dour men in oilskins empty the nets. Amidst the wreckage
of the sea-bed (Anemones, Corals, Sea Fans etc) pour deep-
water Sharks, Hagfish, Toothfish, all lifeless as stone. But these
dripping gargoyles are mostly by-catch—bye-bye catch—
collateral damage chucked back in the brine. And so on, and
so on, trawling for protein, the crewel work of nets…

Reap without sowing,
sleep without knowing…

Byzantine or blind the system, where committees regard a species as if sole, going it alone—no predators nor prey. With half-baked data, they present Stargazy pies, leaving flocks of politicians to squawk over crumbs. Total Allowable Catches? Better an empty sea than a lost election!

> *Reap without sowing,*
> *sleep without knowing...*

Modern oceans going under. Like shopping malls on Christmas Day, they show a twisted, monocultured sort of Life— explosions of Jellyfish, toxic Algal blooms, flesh-eating Microbes, slime-covered beaches—new unnatural histories, now the Fish have been removed.

Reap without sowing,
sleep without knowing...

Once upon a time there were big mamas and papas, hosts of giant Cod who lived until their forties—now they're tiddlers battered by chippies. (Crisp golden skins hide a multitude of sins....)

> *Reap without sowing,*
> *sleep without knowing...*

Lobsters are all that Porthmellin men have to content them; but in Newlyn or St. Ives boats still land a little *Pilchardus sardina*. Barely large fry, they never qualify as 'Pilchards'. Still, who wants school-dinner swimming in tomato sauce? No, let's rebrand it for the modern palate! Styled with parsley sprigs beside its tarnished eye, behold the Cornish Sardine—o sing its praises....

The Accomplice

Methylene blue like alcopops
preferred by bewitched girls, who croon
I'm going to drink myself to death—

and acrid enough to strip out nasal hair
just by breathing nearby—it was the anti-freeze
that sparked a row one time.

Black-ice on the roads, we're passing fields
of low-growing crucifers singed by frost
(their foliage like blackened toes of Arctic explorers)

and I'm watching wipers streak
the foul liquid back and forth across the screen,
fuming at these tides and tributaries,

this run-off flicked away.
Inwardly I curse you for making me
accomplice to this drive-by poisoning

of the Greater Being;
and from the boiling stew inside my gut,
I want you to stop,

to release me into the bitter air,
a pointy-fingered harpy
shrieking with wild recriminations.

But where would you go? You ask.
I'd find somewhere—in woods, or under a hedge!
Laughing softly, you continue

on your route of squeaky reason;
and from the verge the frost mocks me,
glittering teeth on every stump and leaf.

Ice, an Elegy

The Ice Queen is leaving—
all around, her ancient kingdom
is cracking up—trickling, splitting,
as her vast, crystal sleigh
grinds on the fast-track to oblivion.

For millennia she held her huge mirror
steady to the Sun; now she's losing her cool,
sheets shrinking, her albedo body
pocked with melting pools, moulins
milling in, chutes of water sailing her
the slipway of lost forever.

Yet each day her belly calves
desperate bergs of ice. Bereft, these tongues
curl and shrink as they sense their mother
spent—her skin once tinted blue,
now deathly pale.

Her courtiers and creatures
are disappearing too—
in despair they throw their arms into the air;
tall maidens
once yoked in lustrous bridal gowns,
stagger
one by one
to their knees,
faces crashing down
in mounds into the sea.

Even the glacial snow men,
who plucked boulders and carried

their erratic cargo across continents,
now stumble, retreat—valleys scoured
by their dark rheumatic wake.

Everywhere Foxes, Bears,
Wolverines and Leopards mourn their Queen—
prowling the rosaries of paternoster lakes,
they murmur eulogies and prayers.

And at last we hurry in
with tools, instruments and measuring rods
to probe, extend our senses—
to scientize this demise of ice.

Pantoum on Planting Seeds

How I misjudge these smallest things—
dull and dry as peppercorns,
when in my palm I hold
a potency waiting to be sown.

Dull and dry as peppercorns
and yet in dormancy they breathe,
potency waiting to unfold,
sensing fertile sun and soil.

And yet in dormancy they breathe
and slowly awaken—
sensing fertile sun and soil—
to rise with levity and purpose.

Slowly I awaken
to these living beings I hold;
seeking levity and purpose
they whisper, electric with potential.

Addressing the Wild Arum

1. January

Hedges unadorned, beaten by iron-willed blasts. Days scarcely drawing out, and little else points the way when you pioneer your dark green arrow-heads. Perhaps it's hope that raises your repoussé surface, the promise of a new culture? Light flirts with shadows by your chased veins, but the flecks on Wake Robin are the hallmarks of birth.

2. May

When Birds ring the air with the lively warmth of Africa, you're the exotic dancer of the woods. In supple shade at Beltane, you don a waxen cowl—but still you can't conceal your pintle, or how Moth Flies get hooked on your stink. With secret hairs you trap them in your sheath, where they madden, dust up your lips. In moonlight your flesh is luminous, pulsating. Lords and Ladies dance as one.

3. September

The Sun's half past its zenith and Barleycorn sports whiskers. On thickened stalks your berries go green through amber, end as scarlet baubles. Once your tubers were dried for starch—Elizabethan faces set in stiffly petalled ruffs—or were powdered to disguise freckles. We, who rub your parts, are blistered with your poison; yet Mice seek your fruits when frost nips the air. As ripeness dies away, you're Starchwort, and roots hold your worth.

American Rose

For N

A Rose you admire, white, mystical,
dewed with *aldicarb, tedion, bravo*—

how could angels live
in this realm of matter

where nearly all we touch
is branded by the devil?

'The Underneath Farmers'

The cut worm forgives the plow —William Blake

They especially like the rain—
it drums on clods and furrows
and draws them up like ruddy shoots
to roll and wallow in the damp.

When the tractor rumbles overhead
drizzling pellets in tick-tack formation,
it drives them up to dance for God,
to writhe in fields of paradise.

Instead the limpid pools sting and burn
and their skin is quickly turning fuchsia;
they have no hands to wave,
nor tongues to speak,
but their heads and tails are curling,
asking for mercy, begging us to stop.

In Good Hands

You see these, she says,
hands rising into the lamplight
from her shadowed lap,
their easy coupling
parted for a while—

palms up, her fingers stick out,
callused, knobbled at every joint,
like Willows pollarded for years.
In each hand's basin, lines with tributaries
are like streams viewed from high in the hills;
the backs speckled Blackbird eggs,
nails horned as Donkey's hooves.
Fearless hands that grasped Nettles
(*if you hold your breath they won't sting*);
that saved seeds, grubbed
in the woods for Pignuts;
picked Rosehips, Blackberries,
and never mind the scratches;
snipped Betony from the waysides,
slipping stems into mossy pockets,
to wind them out again, fresh as water
from a well. Those constant hands
that cored Liberty, Spartans, Pippins;
delved in dough; raced pies
from the oven; that fed the Birds,
darned, soothed, rubbed olive oil
into the raw, new skins of babies;
made haphazard hospital corners;
put out huge House Spiders
and Small Tortoiseshells; laid Cowslips
on the graves of village people—

Like this. Her fingers interlock
to form the church without the steeple.
In our Earth everything fits together just so.

Wide-eyed I stared at their craggy surface
that settled back into her lap
as if in silent prayer. In good hands
I learned to cherish every living being.

Green Drift

There is no force in the world but love. —Rilke

Crawling into bed like a peasant,
with mud-grained feet, soil under the nails
of my toes—but too tired to care—
the heaviness of the day's exertions draws

my body downward—each muscle and bone
finding its bliss—and I close my eyes
on a green panorama, shades of every
nuance, the contours of leaves in high

definition. A film encoded on the visual cortex,
I observe again those lanceolate shapes, the forage silk
which slipped between our fingers and thumbs
(still redolent with that Ramson scent),

the mounding herbage that we plucked,
backs bent as in a Van Gogh study.
Behind my eyelids, vernal waves rise and fall,
hymn of this community to which my senses flock—

ancient rite of magnetic Birds, Dionysus riding me,
greens rushing on the inside of my eyelids,
mosaics of foliage, fingers ablaze with Nettle stings,
soles still alive to the narrow woodland path,

its vertebrae of roots, pad of compressed earth.
High on Spring, I'm a biophile
and incurable; nor would I care for any cure—
would only be a node in Great Mother's body

where, drifting into the canopy of sleep, I see foliar veins
close-up—illumined as if by angels—
feel the breathing of stomata. Then, like a drunken Bee,
I surrender to this divine inebriation.

Wallpaper

And there are the moments that it all fades
into a background of flourishes and waves—

not just the repeated patterns of branches,
the prints on water when the wind dances,

flowers whose heads function for vases,
or ornamental birds set behind bars;

but the dappled copper defining the Beech,
the silvers of a Birch being all that we perceive.

Then we are sealed up—rain an inconvenience;
mountains an obstruction; the atmosphere venal;

and when even the Moon and stars are for sale,
our minds roll ever tighter within their cellophane.

Best Paper

Briskness often met my request—
a knife set down, a task on hold,
hands wrung through and through her apron;

and tailing her quick-march into the study,
air regulated by curtains,
a grandmother clock's steady insistence,
I'd watch her shut the bureau's flap
and see the bottom drawer yawn wide.

As if poking through her old trousseau,
where hopes pinched like narrow slingbacks,
my mother would unfold an envelope,
draw out a creamy sheaf—two or three sheets—
dealt onto my palms.

Back with my scatter of crayons,
I'd sit awed by these white windows,
how they could open onto marvellous worlds,
landscapes with fabled wizards and creatures;

then holding one up to the light
I'd find the watermark—
that imprint of the conqueror astride his Horse,
spear poised to charge a Basilisk,
its reptile body hidden in the grains of snow.

Best paper was always rationed out—
just those few folios of bond
to make a birthday or a Christmas card;
it focussed my attention,
made each pencil-stroke an offering
to the Paper God.

Frugality also convinced my mother
to visit jumble sales,
save bottle-tops and foil
in aid of Guide Dogs for the Blind.

Nor was she alone in hoarding rubber bands and things
in old tobacco tins—
our neighbour Joan boiled up crusts of soap,
bestowed her daughter's hand-me-downs.

But I grew up wedding myself
to malls and high-street chains;
that war-time scrimping felt anachronistic in an age
when gratifying each whim became
The Way to Happiness;

and I knew nothing of the costs—
a string of novelties and greetings cards,
a world of saturated gloss.

The Cancer

The current financial stripping of economies and environments across the world exhibits... all the hallmark characteristics of a carcinogenic invasion. —John McMurtry

A cell grows, mutates, divides, and multiplies—power-surging life, evolved with no primordial forces at core, but primogenital rights an inner lore. From the stimuli of discovery, to have, to own, a form previously unknown, which bursts into Superbeing, hungers for more.

And still senescence has no check, no regulatory effect, so that Growth becomes the goal, becomes immortalized—this strange apotheosis of mind, a selfish strand that science gives most credence to; that state mythologies expand.

And isn't this just spring, sempiternal summer—nature without her fickle change? Just like it's human nature to seek to better the self; to have everything sunny-side up? To crawl, to stand, walk on two legs above all four-legged forms? To have power over, recreate the self over and over—metastasized past the confines of a single body?

Meanwhile Greed gains ground—on and on, jaws breaking mountains to serve the purpose of itself. Head buried in the earth's febrile breast, it sucks out every ounce, but never asks, *what next?*

The Longest Day

I crouch in the wet heat
opaque with its furred slick of suds,
(this intimacy of our husbanding
resources), my body stiff
from overwork, ball-bearings
studded on the inside of my brow.
My sigh is involuntary—
I'm wrecked, mind rutted
like an old drovers' track
at Midsummer—these dripping digits
that served to strike the laptop keys,
this head, these naked limbs not
the temple
to which my higher self aspires.
No, I'm the steeplejack stuck on the job;
the paratrooper dangling in Sainte-Mère-Église,
my parachute tangled on the point
where matter yearns for spirit.
I want you to help me, and I call out—
you're a damp, tousled angel
come to soap my neck and back
with strokes that draw me down
to Earth, submerge me in your sea.
I sink below the surface
so that eyes, nose, mouth
are a Pacific island breathing steam.
Beneath I'm a diver rocked
by sounds the foetus makes
trying its lungs inside the womb.
Now I'm nothing
but this steady breathing;
eyes focussed on the white

expanse of ceiling; mind washed
of all the day's dogged drive,
work matters not a jot.
My gaze is long, unflinching—
as air and water slowly
I'm returning.

From *Greenwash: a User's Manual*

When it's that really tough
competitive edge you're after,
just front-load your business
into our new green
washing machine;

it takes all kinds—
and at high or low temperatures
will tackle the most stubborn
campaigns, offsetting your conscience
instantly—top results our guarantee!

Our washer uses only
the most charismatic of powders,
and will even take delicates,
like oil companies, airlines
and car manufacturers—

creating a soft-soap screen,
a turn-coat of iridescent suds,
in which your CEO can parade
transparent on the stock exchange.

Not that this
is the emperor's new clothes—
after a rinse with softener
(for that added shareholder comfort),
and plenty of extra spin,

your business will be newly laundered.
It can then be hung out to dry
(for that natural fresh-air scent)—

you secure in the knowledge
that it's had a cleaner,
greener type of wash.

Lament for Baiji, Yangtze River Dolphin

Our People's Republic's opened like a giant
red flower—head looking West—
and ever since our world's been turning sour.

Along the Yangtze a filthy stream
of traffic pours—dredgers, barges, tourist
boats tossing our sampans aside.

They say it's the way forward,
but this great river's giving up the ghost—
and with no Fish or Shrimps to eat,
our River Dolphin's vanished.

*

On the fifth day of the fifth month
our hut inspired hopeful aromas;
and women came with ruby thread to tie
Bamboo leaves round homemade dumplings.

Pang was rosy-cheeked, scolding me
for my despondent moods. As usual we'd honour
Qu Yang, our patriotic poet—his *Lament for Ying*
and drowning in the river.

Legend tells that fishermen threw dumplings in
to tempt the River Dragons from the poet's body;
but we believe our sleek Baiji came clicking,
whistling him away.

Cheer up, Huang! Pang urged me.
Soon young men with boats and drums
will sound the Dragon's heart.

Soon after Duan Wu the Sun attains its peak
and we need the rains to plant our rice;
last year they didn't come—for months the soil
was bones boiled and set like glue.

But this is Duan Wu in Golden Pig year,
Pang persisted;
Dragons will surely bring the rains!

Father smoked and watched her wrap the sticky parcels,
his face a haze of bluish mist;
he remembered the Great Leap Forward,
how Mao denounced the tales that kept our Dolphin safe.

Superstitious maybe, but old men like Father
would never hunt them for their flesh. *Those who hurt Baiji
are always cursed,* he said.

*

Now Pang patches trousers—
her sewing brings a little income;
she sighs and glances up. In the wintry light
her face looks drawn, aged.

My wife become a stranger!
I search my thoughts for something
to restore her cheerful smile—
a little joke, a reminiscence?

But hunger's gnawing at my belly
and I've no strength to break the silence;
this year even Golden Pig was out of luck—
the rains arrived, but heavier than we'd ever known.

How long we'll survive
lies with the gods—
perhaps no longer than our flower can,
its heart devoured by its head?

Media Story

Dalek generation can't tell a Bee
from a Wasp. Today's children are more likely
to know a brand of shoe than a leaf.

The Future Gazes Back

After Anthony Gormley's 'Amazonian Field', an installation comprising approx 24,000 figures, exhibited at The Royal Academy, 2010

They creep through the Palladian
door-cases, nudging our giant feet;

I daren't bend and touch—
after all this *is* Art, and the attendant is wary
as a Bloodhound in a manger—

but I imagine dank clay
(that strange way a corpse feels).

With limbless forms, they seem ready-
shrouded, as if buried upright in their thousands,
the mass production of a late Chinese Emperor—

yet these the funerary statues of our great
grandchildren, if we don't change.

Out of place their folksiness, perhaps,
in the former Senate Room of London University,
its glazed lunettes, painted stucco and *putti?*

Eyes hollowed out, the raw vision
of every manikin makes us want to pocket one,

adopt him/her as an act of redemption.
Instead we avert our gaze,
degrees of complicity needling our minds

as we stand against the edifice
that's made us who we are—

shades of Bacon, Newton, Hume, Locke,
stories of a world
running out against the clock.

Vermin Acts

From the Parish Records, Cranborne, Dorset, 1703

Bounty on the heads of 1 dozen Rooks
paid to one Samuel Gord,

four pence.

Bounty on the heads of 1 Polecat
& 18 dozen Sparrows paid to one William Toms,

three shillings & four pence.

Bounty on the heads of 3 Hedgehogs
paid to one George Lardon,

six pence.

Bounty on the heads of 13 Bullfinches
paid to one Joseph Cook,

a shilling & one pence.

Bounty on the heads of 1 Stoat, 1 Hawk
& 4 Hedgehogs paid to one John Millar,

a shilling.

Bounty on the heads of 27 Choughs
& 3 dozen Sparrows paid to one Thomas Clark,

a shilling & three pence.

Bounty on the heads of 9 Jays & 1 Buzzard
paid to the very same Thomas Clark,

eleven pence.

Bounty on the head of 1 Fox
paid to one John Warden,

a shilling.

Bounty on the heads of 2 Stoats
paid to one William Pain,

four pence.

(Perhaps out of all these men
William may have winced as
he wrung the little skulls from
their spines?)

For ringing the church bells at Easter
paid to the ringers,

two shillings.

(Note: all bounties paid in
accordance with Her Majesty's
statute.)

capitalism, a Sonnet

chemical Macaque   glaxosmithkline
roche   trepanned-brain Baboon

max factor eyes burning Cat   l'oreal
Rabbit   (the devil wears perfume)

o, dear   easyjet   ryanair
melting Reindeer, Polar Bear

but a bargain for mcdonalds—
Earth's rainforests   slashed

as Asians sweat for adidas
nike   the evil empire's goddess

o, bless all ecocidal patriarchs—so smart
in suits   armani uniforms

a cocktail of intellect and greed
hellish stuff   they puppet us to need

The Sky on Guy Fawkes Night

Is peppered with shot—
as if the stars had been fired
from their sockets.

     (Out there it could be down-town Basra…)

A stink of sulphur in their pockets
teenage kicks rush about,
banging up the city;

while all the families down the Rec
are herded behind barriers
to get their fix of

shock and awe

at raining explosions—

     HELLFIRE   ACID BLAST   PRETTY KILLER—

and standing by in hi-viz coats
pro utilitate hominum
St John Ambulance,
with steaming mugs of jollity.

Strange this good-humour
when dioxins and particulates
fuzz the air—

an alien invasion
received with riotous applause.

On a Single Hand

I count the things which connect me to him;
my fingers on the straps, the brass latch—

his old briefcase, tan leather scuffed, scratched,
a buckle broken, sides split open

like a slackened mouth. I take my needle,
pull the rotten stitching from the holes,

begin the task of making good. It'd been my father's
from his accounting days, before the management

consultant phase when he switched to a black
snap-shut case with combination lock.

Years later, while the banks were going bust,
he lay bubbling at the lips as if drowning in paralysis.

I used to insist that Marx predicted this
(I mean the economic crash). Now I caressed the skin

where he still had some feeling; I'd barely touched him
since I was a child—and now there was only this.

Around us nurses, porters, cleaners went about their business,
and overhead *Nil by Mouth* was a sign on death row.

Cancer was eating him up, thickening his blood,
causing strokes; but no one would admit he was dying—

each afternoon the physios wheeled him
to the gym for 'Rehabilitation'.

I push my needle in, draw it out;
it hurts my fingers and the threads get tangled,

but I work at it—
this case will slowly brim with poems.

Compost

The Dharma is like an Avocado!
Some parts so ripe you can't believe it,
      —from 'Avocado', Gary Snyder

It was turning time,
and from the shed
where Wood Mice ride out Winter,
I took the weathered fork,
rolled up my sleeves,
set to work.
It always intrigues me to see
what becomes of carrot-flaps,
squeeze-weary bags of tea,
daily coffee grounds
(though they already look like soil),
or hair balls teased from the bristles of a brush.
Even the regular peaks of egg-boxes,
and the skin-boats that float
the pistachio-flesh of Avocados,
are reduced to black sugo sauce—
a fine tilth, like mindfulness.
But what about that *great, big round seed*,
surely it remained hard, intractable?
Once I scooped one out and potted it
in the garden centre's best peat-free stuff,
then placed it in the Sun,
and watered it from time to time.
It never budged,
but that turning day
another came to light,
curled amidst the warming heap
where Protozoa
perform their transmutations.

The seed had split through the middle,
lay naked like a pair of cream-skinned buttocks
sprouting a pale green tumescence—
just like my Buddha nature,
my own most growing part.

Strange Fruits

Few could conceive of venturing out after dark,
forehead glowing in the murk like a deep-sea diver,
and swimming patiently the length of the lawn,
pot and stick in hand to harvest the ripening beasts
that appear from deep in the undergrowth to feed.

Yet there's an acquired taste that comes with surveying
the most intimate corners of the night-time garden—
the meeting of Woodlice, the greeting of Earwigs;
being for the Moths a mini-lunar magnet; and
stooping low over Lettuce seedlings, the strange

acrobats I spy hanging—brown Berthas with orange frills;
and curling from the ravaged Mizuna, soft cream slippers,
tortoiseshell buns, and the sleek, black moustaches
which are the heavy-weights of this nocturnal circus—
each coaxed from its trapeze and gathered

for displacement in a far-flung hedge or field.
Hearing of my nightly excursions, you extol the sheer
convenience of killing—those pellets left like grey scat
beside the Lupins. Still Birds find their fruits wherever
they fall, and isn't it the dead that taste strangest of all?

Monsoon June

After the Christian Aid advert depicting a South Asian woman up to her neck in water, with the caption—*Do us a favour will you? Write to your MP about that climate change bill!*

The water's encircling my neck, Kali—
a damp strangle like the hands of my brother,
when he's too drunk to know better.
And these rags I called a sari
are wings trailing in these fields-turned-sea
that flap me up to rooftops, bridges
where we perch with our dry-lipped children, waiting.

Sometimes when darkness laps at our feet
and the Moon throws us silver shackles,
I lie awake, wishing your four arms would pincer me away,
prize my skull among the garlands
that chatter from your breasts
as you dance the charnel-grounds with Lord Shiva.

But I must be strong for all our little ones;
and so each day I wade with my hollow-bellied vessel—
like a girl trying to swim, her float so buoyant—praying
you'll speed my return—the long, long way from the pump,
clean water leaden on my head.

The stench I can accept, the bloated corpses, flooding
sewage—but keep those scaly Muggers snoozing in their lairs
now their hunting grounds are everywhere.
And yes, I do seek protection, dear Durga,
though I've made no offerings—the usual ball of rice
and flowers—but we have nothing now,
and the plants are drowned.

Archana says the villages of Maharashta come last
for handouts because the newsmen never visit—
they stay in Mumbai where sacred Cows
are floating in the streets.

The holy men believe these are the heaviest rains
India's known in all her history—
in the city many houses have no light, telephone, or water
from the tap. And so perhaps we're lucky?
When rains sweep the world away,
we know how to live on the edge.

Cherry Picking

Back in Blighty the rain's relentless—everyone's dying
for a *proper* Summer. In June we always pick cherries,
but this year they've split open. Like torn mouths
they bleed—hang rotting from the trees.

Tonglen

After Pema Chodron

Dark pool of anger, grief, pain—
breathing in
kinship
with the suffering of all beings;

silver shoal of smiles, gratitude, joy,
breathing out
blessings—
may all beings know they too are Love.

East Mendip Mapping

In the cold valley so compelling
this strange white lapping
was a rain-soaked map
with wind swelling—
Ordnance Survey
front to back
around my hand
wrapping.

I lifted it—
sapped and pale,
mud a natural feature—
and it raised a limp sail
that filled with air,
was soon a kite that trailed
Lullington, Frome, Nunney,
inches rising fast to miles.

Folds blown out,
this insurgent mapping
had thrown off its creases,
defied a return to neat concertinas;
and unfettered edges flapping
was taking on the hill,
the rain clapping—
slipway,
tearaway,
bundle it up.

*

Now the Mendips rise
with new folds and ridges;
Little Wood is lost,
and the Fosse is crossed
with unforeseen contours.

Useless,
with Castle Cary crumpled;
yet fibres that were pulped and fixed
recall at last the nature of the names:

Waterlip,
Withybrook,
Winterwell Lane.

Nativity

For Glennie Kindred

To mark it, there will be no tree
on a claw behind the neat settee—
a calvary where it will bleed
and lose its crown of needles.

No, she'll welcome in Midwinter's dark
with prunings from the garden—
stems of Willow, Beech and Birch
sucking water from a jar—

give thanks as they bud and turn
new leaves for the Sun's rebirth.

The Knife

They have made me
a knife—

not a weapon,
but a tool to handle
expectation,
judgment,
the rough bark
of commands,
the moral platitudes
they'd crowd
in dull acidic soil.

They've made me
a tempered blade

to whittle Life
down to its green fibres,
to cleave a rod of truth,
with which to stand
witness to the rain,

the sincerity of Nature—

they've made me
a cutting
edge.

The Vigil

1.
The night you'd been castrated, we lay on the floor,
your lacklustre spine cushioned by my spoon.

Groggy still from anaesthetic, you'd attempt to lift your head,
reach the stitched-up wound, but I'd push you down,

anxious that you wouldn't lick the shrunken sack
where for months the testes grew—

ebony eggs coupled under wisps of sandy fur
that fringed your lower belly.

All through the night we lay there, kept apart
by veils of muslin sleep through which I'd stir

at your every twitch and broken whimper.
It felt like a betrayal, what I'd let them do—

and yet, your life had from the beginning been out
of your control. A feisty, independent spirit

harnessed, brought out on a lead, which kept you close
to heel—a prisoner-possession.

Had you been a mixed blessing? At times
when you disobeyed or ran away, you'd unleash a depth

charge of fury I never knew I owned. But there were joyous
moments too—you, sprawled on your back,

giddy, playful, your tiny member popping out,
an infant curio. And I, kneeling above,

smiling at your crooked grin, felt your muddy eyes
which could only blink, wind me again

into that labyrinth of human, of animal,
where I'd grasp nascent love, trust,

that miscellany of sounds, gestures, habits
which would grow our bond.

2.
See how you loved chasing balls, but annoyingly preferred
being chased with one clamped between your jaws;

how you'd hang onto a toy with such strength
I could lift you clean off the floor. (I'd tire first.)

See how you'd run on three legs, as if a hind one
were injured (but on inspection wasn't);

how you'd dig through the compost heap
on the scent of rodents. (What would I have done if you'd
ever caught one?)

See how when you heard the bath-tub filling,
you'd hide behind the sofa, need coaxing out,

and how afterwards you'd run around the house
dementedly—as if you couldn't stand the dog shampoo.

See how you often startled at your farts,
and belched loudly after meals;

how you'd curl beneath my desk,
chin resting on my feet. (Comforting for chilblains.)

See how you grew too big for your boots,
and barked at passing trucks, lorries.

See how of all your nicknames, you best lived up to
'Houdini'…

The Never-never Land

On Ecological Debt Day, September 23rd, 2008

Planet in the red, we've pawned our Great Mother. For tomorrow's reserves—forests, fish, topsoil, minerals—we're indebted to our children. They themselves will live on Mars, reading *Peter Pan*.

Marginal, iii

Nyn ges gûn heb legas,
na kei heb scovern.

There is no down without an eye,
nor hedge that cannot hear.

Modern Magus

Silbury Hill, 5th July 2009

For Ken

Cupped by the land, the massive Neolithic pap. From its peak, the night-watch sees bubbles of light floating over the field. To the modern magus, it's a sign of a supernatural circle, and the news is instantly diffused, bounced off the satellites of cell phone corporations. Dawn brings crocodilian aircraft droning overhead, snapping up their aerial pix; more will follow with hordes of serial spotters.

On the ground, the form's hazy in our minds as we climb the barbed-wire fence. In deference to the farmer's crop, the procession ants through tram-lines cut in waves of regulated green (a hollow in our hearts for Yellow Rattle, Cornflowers, Poppies.)

At the threshold of the temple, the Sun beats the circle silver, and Skylarks offer molten jubilations. We bend to slip off shoes and socks and feet flow over the bowed stems of corn, feel it thick as rush matting. But this alone cannot explain these strange sensations, tingling energy that electrifies our bodies.

Is this what brings us pilgrims? This frisson of mystery in a world irrationally dogmatic? Devotees douse with rods or practise Chi Gong; others sit in small vortices drumming and chanting into the mystical tattoo. All around the corn wavers, twitching its ears.

Sacré Coeur

Top of the old nonconformist chapel
the eighth flat is our temple. You climb stairs
into white expanses where my arms stretch out,
and we soften, grow wings on Jacob's Ladder.

Our sanctuary, from where all Summer
we'd survey terracotta roofs
and white-washed walls, make-believe the cobbled hill
had brought us to Montmartre;

and lying there, on Paris linen sheets,
would see the Sun fold and press its face
on the arched chapel windows, trying to part
the curtains, peeping in.

Now Autumn—
in the courtyard the stately Hawthorn
is stoic through these shortening days
and sudden frosts; lays itself bare
as I seek the first threads of light.

Coiling up the kitchen-blind, I coax the Sun
through every angle on its East to South axis—
tilt my face upwards like a leaf,
drawing radiance into each particle and cell;

feel how it forms warm pools in the cold room,
jewels and dries the condensation
on all the glass panes.
Ah, this gift of passive solar heating—

we lovers silhouetted in our light-box
reading *Sun of gOd*, send supplications
to Lugh—trace the shrinking arcs of his arms
as Earth tips us towards Winter.

Some days, when clouds stubborn the town,
I consider the Sun's constancy, the fiery corona
brimming above all; then my spirit rises out
over the rooftops, soars higher than the late Swifts

upward through moist layers of gas,
dirigible, a shiny-faced bubble—warm, cold, warm—
seeking the troposphere, the stratosphere,
where jets scar the Earth's aura.

At last, when I'm no longer a speck—
more molten than Icarus—I look back in awe
at the consequence of that love—o Sun,
o sacred heart.

Cunt Magic

This gap in the hedge
is neither absence nor lack

but a green Moon—the frame
around the young Wheat beyond,

a heavenly gateway
that beckons us to quit the path,

its stiles and bridleways,
the blue willow-patterns of our thought,

and pass through this cunicle,
this cunning—finger its tender flowers,

its pitted stems, feel frissons
of what we once knew as holy.

Thereafter trust that the Bird *not*
in the hand is worth a cunctipotence

in the bush, and reawaken the desire
for Life's wild fecundity.

Marginal, iv

Jew's Ear—on Elders
a living slur—glistens with
fresh indignation.

Climbing out of a Dog Eat Dog World

*There is nothing in the world, I would venture to say, that would so
effectively help one to survive even the worst conditions as the knowledge
that there is a meaning in one's life.* —Viktor Frankl

There's this fear in growing up that your parents' genes
will one day kick in. And perhaps they already have.

I'm a human body, a personality, and also a soul. As such
I tell myself I've chosen this pain. Why else would I be here

as the Planet's heating up, if not to speak of the Holocaust
we've launched on this universal jewel—

Earth-Life unique with its Goldilocks conditions?
So many creatures lighting out—Yuman Box Turtle,

Caspian Tiger, Paradise Parrot, Golden Toad—
I cradle your dark spaces as rainforests dwindle,

and painted Kayapo people march for living rivers, trees—
these natural riches they steward for their children;

men, women, so proud and strong, yet almost naked
in the midst of the rushing, wasted city.

What can a poet do? Bear witness; be a conscience, perhaps?
Sometimes I feel such agony to see what ignorance and greed

are snuffing out. Yet somehow I find the inner rungs to climb
from despair. Hand over hand, there's always something

to learn. Love is my meaning—through it I'm sure of nothing
but a personal evolution. Darwinists may reject this notion;

but in this life-time I know I'm evolving—as I have in others before. Maybe I'll manage more than my parents ever could.

Now I notice when my heart has closed. Only the heart breaks patterns of fear. Together we can make a Being Love Being world.

Time-out, Black-out

For Earth Hour

Sitting quietly as if no one were at home,
in candlelight our faces morph, shadows fly,
we breathe in the silence and our pulses slow,

unplug, disengaging from the charge that throws
the box, the red-eyed Cyclops off stand-by.
You and I are quiet, as if we were alone—

no phone, no gadgets, no kinetic motion
humming, whirring all the time—
and breathe in the silence till our pulses slow

the treadmill, at a standstill the revolving doors
so nothing moves, shut down all production lines.
We sit quietly, the ending unknown,

while across the land steely rows of scaffolds
no longer hold the buzz that plies our wires;
breathing in the silence our pulses slow,

the lights go out across the globe
as all the Earth respires.
We wait quietly, now very much at home;
breathing in the silence, our faces glow.

Today, of All Days

In memory of Annette Tolson

Today a Hare leaps from the shadows of a thicket;
I'm its silent, motionless observer,
its ear-erect alertness, its wide eyeball watch.

Today shafts of Winter sunlight rouse me—
hair-tips stretching up to bathe
in its pale, ultra-violet tint.

Today the Oak's roots support me;
through its cleft and curvy leaves I breathe,
knotted arms crowning my dependence.

Today a crew of Rooks fly up
from tree-tops in gregarious, airy lifting;
I'm their co-arising everywhere.

Today the wind blows from the North;
I stand by my door—sense how Spirit
lives inside this house of bone.

Today thousands of Mycelia connect me,
by sugared strands invisibly through the soil;
I fruit browny-white; deliquesce here, there, nowhere.

Notes

The Worst Winter in Thirty Years
Two recent British winters (2009 & 10), which have been unusually cold compared with previous years, have led elements of the tabloid media to assert that this proves that global warming is a myth. However, global warming requires evidence of global trends, and a report in *The Independent* ('What the weather is telling us', 14.1.2011) explains this well: "2010 was a particularly extreme year, with record-breaking snowstorms in Europe and the US, an unprecedented heat-wave in Russia, and floods across the globe from Pakistan to Tennessee... two leading U.S. monitors of global weather revealed that 2010 was the hottest and wettest yet recorded. And it was the 34th year running that global temperatures have been above the 20th-century average.... Nine of the ten warmest years on record have occurred since 2001. The warmer it gets the more unpredictable the weather will be.... It is beyond dispute that the Earth has been warming for decades. The vast majority of climate scientists believe that is because we are releasing gases which trap heat inside our atmosphere. The level of carbon dioxide we produce has almost doubled since the Industrial Revolution."

The Unsung Pilchard
Manannan, Celtic god of the sea; musyk, a Revived Late Cornish word for drizzle; Porthmellin, Mullion Cove; traine oil, oil from pressed Pilchards used to light Cornish lamps; huer, look-out man for Pilchard schools; quilkins, Cornish for Frog; scrowlers, Cornish dialect for Pilchards; stems, here, refers to lanes drawn from the coastline out to sea, where fishermen were granted fishing rights. For much of my research about industrial fishing, I must acknowledge Professor Callum Roberts' excellent study, *The Unnatural History of the Sea.*

Addressing the Wild Arum
Frequent in hedge bases, *Arum maculatum* has various common names, including Cuckoo-pint, Lords and Ladies, Starchwort, Wake Robin and Willy-lily.

American Rose
A United Nations' International Labor Organization study in 2000 showed that 60% of rose workers in Ecuador suffered from

headaches, blurred vision, muscular twitching and other symptoms of pesticide poisoning. Ecuador is a major exporter of roses to the US, especially around Valentine's Day.

'The Underneath Farmers'
The phrase is borrowed from Harry Martinson's poem 'The Earthworm', translated from the Swedish by Robert Bly.

Lament for Baiji, Yangtze River Dolphin
After Qu Yang, an ancient Chinese poet whose death is marked at Duan Wu, the Dragon Boat Festival, when zongzi dumplings are traditionally made.

capitalism, a Sonnet
Ecocidal, from ecocide. For more details see: www.thisisecocide.com

Marginal, iii
A Cornish proverb.

Lightning Source UK Ltd.
Milton Keynes UK
UKOW050801300612

195266UK00001B/46/P